CONTEMPORARY'S ACTIVITY-BASED EMPLOYMENT PROGRAM

You're Hired!

Book Two: Getting the Right Job

Marilyn Clark
John Mahaffy
Michael St. John
Jan Hart Weihmann

Project Editor
Sarah Conroy

Consultant
Maryann D. Sakamoto
Assistant Principal/Adult Education
Atlantic County Vocational School
Mays Landing, New Jersey

CB
CONTEMPORARY
BOOKS
CHICAGO

Library of Congress Cataloging-in-Publication Data

You're hired!

    Contents: bk. 1. Charting your career path —
bk. 2. Getting the right job.
    1. Vocational guidance.   I. Clark, Marilyn.
HF3581.Y69   1991   650.14   91-23647
ISBN 0-8092-4031-9 (v. 1)
ISBN 0-8092-4030-0 (v. 2)

Photo Credits: p. 1—© Publications Services/The
University of Illinois at Chicago; pp. 2, 22, 35, 53,
80—© C. C. Cain Photography, Inc.; p. 21—© David
Frazier/Tony Stone Worldwide; p. 39—© John Colwell/
Grant Heilman Photography; p. 65—© Frank Siteman/
Gartman Agency; p. 79—© Spencer Grant/Gartman
Agency

Published by Contemporary Books, Inc.
Two Prudential Plaza, Chicago, Illinois 60601-6790
Manufactured in the United States of America
International Standard Book Number: 0-8092-4030-0

Editorial Director
Caren Van Slyke

Editorial
Mark Boone
Betsy Rubin
Jane Samuelson
Lisa Black
Robin O'Connor
Lisa Dillman
Laura Larson

Editorial Assistant
Erica Pochis

Editorial Production Manager
Norma Fioretti

Production Editor
Jean Farley Brown

Production Assistant
Marina Micari

Cover Design
Georgene Sainati

Cover Illustrator
Linda Kelen

Illustrator
Graziano, Krafft & Zale, Inc.

Art & Production
Carolyn Hopp
Sue Springston

Typography
Ellen Yukel

Photo Research
Sheryl Mersfelder

Photography
C. C. Cain

Contents

To the Student

This is the second of two books in the series *You're Hired!* The first book, *Charting Your Career Path*, focused on learning about yourself and deciding which jobs might be for you. If you completed Book One, you know about some jobs that interest you. If you did not complete Book One, talk with your teacher.

Book Two, *Getting the Right Job*, will help you learn more about jobs that interest you. It also will show you how to find and keep a job that's right for you.

 ## Getting the Right Job

Once you know what job interests you, the next step is getting that job. And after you get the job, you need to know how to succeed at work. This book focuses on your job search and your job success.

What you will learn:

- how to find the information you need
- how to find job openings
- how to write a resume and cover letter
- how to fill out a job application
- how to have a successful interview
- your rights at work
- new words

How you will learn:

- by reading stories and answering questions
- by exploring your community
- by doing job search activities
- by filling out forms

As you work through this book, you should check with your teacher often, to be sure you are on the right track.

Learning About Jobs

You need good **information** to make good choices in life. Before you make a decision about a job choice, it is important to know what the work is really like. You also need to know if the job fits your needs.

In this unit, you will think about what *you* want from a job. Then, you will gather information about the job that interests you most. You will decide whether your job choice meets your needs.

How This Unit Will Help You

A job that is right for you is one that you are likely to keep. If you know more about the work you want to do, you can make better decisions about your life and career.

In this unit you will

- think about what you **want** from a job

- use **resources** to find out what the work is really like

- decide if this work is right for **you**

- choose how to overcome any **barriers**

Juan's Story

Juan García had been a parking-lot attendant for the past three years. He felt that it was time for a change. He wanted to find a new job.

On his day off, he went to the public employment agency in his town. He met a job counselor named Ms. Cook. They talked about the job he had now. They discussed the kind of job he was looking for.

Ms. Cook gave Juan inventories so that he could rate his values, skills, and job interests. Ms. Cook told Juan that his values and skills needed to match his job choice. One job that fit his values and skills was carpentry. He wanted to find out more about it.

Ms. Cook told Juan that he should think about what he needed from a job. He wasn't sure what she meant.

"I just want a better job," Juan said. "Carpentry sounds good to me."

"Yes," Ms. Cook agreed, "but does carpentry really meet your needs? You say you don't like being a parking-lot attendant because the work is done mostly outdoors and doesn't pay much. What about carpentry? You need to find out if it will be right for you."

Juan agreed. These were important issues for him to learn about. Carpentry seemed to meet his values, skills, and interests. But if he didn't like the working conditions, or if it did not pay enough to support his family, it would not be a good job for him after all.

Questions About the Story

1. Where did Juan go to find out about jobs?

   _____

2. What job did Juan have that he no longer wanted?

   _____

3. What job did Juan decide to find out more about?

   _____

4. Does Juan know for sure that carpentry will be a good job for him?

   _____

5. Juan thought carpentry sounded good, but he needed to find out if the work was mostly outdoors. What else did he need to find out?

   _____

   _____

6. Can you think of any other questions that Juan needs to answer before he can be sure about carpentry?

   _____

   _____

What I Want in a Job

Juan had to ask himself what he needed from a job. You also need to think about what *you* need out of a job.

Directions

Step 1. Answer the following questions as honestly as you can.

1. What kind of working conditions do you want in a job?
   Working conditions are where and how you work. Indoors? In a quiet place? In an office? Standing? Sitting? Lifting?

   _____

   _____

   _____

2. What is the starting pay you need?

   _____

3. What kind of benefits do you want in a job?
   Benefits can include health, dental, and eye care; life and disability insurance; and retirement, or pension, plans.

   _____

   _____

   _____

4. Do you want to be able to advance in a job?
   Advance means to move up or be promoted in the job.

   _____

   _____

5. Would you relocate?
   Are you willing to move to another town for a job?

   _____

   _____

6. What do you think you need most in a job?

_____

_____

_____

7. How much education do you want to have?
A job may require a high school diploma, GED, or special certification.

_____

_____

8. Do you want to work full-time or part-time now? In five years?

_____

_____

9. What work schedule do you want to work?
Days? Nights? Swing shift? Weekends?

_____

_____

10. Can you think of anything else that you want from a job?

_____

_____

_____

Step 2. Go back through the list. Circle the numbers of the questions that are **most important** to you.

⬤ Resources

You know *what* you would like to get out of work. Now you will learn *how* to get good information about jobs that interest you.

Below are some **resources** to help you find out more about a job. Resources are things or people that can help you find the information you need.

People
It is very helpful to talk with people who do the kind of work that interests you. Sometimes, you can learn a lot about the job from these people.

The Employment Service
Most towns and cities have an employment service (sometimes called the unemployment office or employment security office). This is a government agency. At the employment service, you can get job counseling and can find information on jobs that interest you. This service is free.

Your Public Library
The public library in your area has helpful information about jobs. If you do not have a public library nearby, you may have to use the local high school or community

college library. A librarian can often help you find what you need. These books, published by the U.S. government, will give you good information on jobs:

- *The Dictionary of Occupational Titles*: This book lists the titles of almost every job in this country.

- *Occupational Outlook Handbook*: This book lists the duties and working conditions for more than 200 jobs.

- *Guide for Occupational Exploration*: This book lists the duties, working conditions, skills, and training and entry requirements for more than 65 types of jobs.

School Job Placement Offices
Most colleges and technical schools have a job placement office (career center). You can often find information about different careers there.

Finding Your Resources

You have many resources to help you learn more about your job interest.

Directions
Step 1. Write your job interest here:

_____

(This should be Job Interest #1, if you have completed Book One.)

Step 2. Answer the following questions about your resources.

1. Can you name a person who knows something about the kind of work your job interest involves?

_____

2. Where is the employment service nearest to you?

address: _____

phone: _____

3. What is the name of the library closest to where you live?

_____

Finding Out About a Job

Juan needed to earn enough money to support his family. He also wanted a job where he could work indoors. He had many questions about carpentry and wanted to talk with a carpenter. By chance, his neighbor was having her kitchen remodeled. Juan asked her if he could leave a message for the carpenter. He included his name and phone number.

Two days later, Juan got a call from Fred Smith, the carpenter. Fred told Juan to come over to the job at lunchtime.

Juan wrote down six questions he wanted to ask Fred. Part of their conversation is shown below.

Juan thanked Fred for his time. He went home and thought about what he had learned. He had not known that carpenters had to buy their own tools. He also had not known that the work was not steady all year round. He was not sure he wanted to be a carpenter. He needed to learn more.

 # Questions

1. Who did Juan find to talk with about carpentry?

_____

2. One of Juan's work values is to find steady work. According to Fred, is carpentry steady work?

_____

3. Juan hopes to find work that is indoors. Does Fred work indoors most of the time?

_____

4. After the conversation, was Juan sure that he wanted to become a carpenter?

_____

5. What do you think Juan should do next?

_____

_____

_____

Answers

1. Fred Smith, a carpenter 2. no 3. no 4. no 5. learn more about carpentry

Using Resources to Learn More

After talking with Fred, Juan wanted to find out more about carpentry. He went to his public library. He asked a librarian to help him find the resources on job information.

Juan found carpentry in the *Occupational Outlook Handbook*. He read about the job. He did not like the tasks and working conditions. It was not steady work, and it was often outdoors.

Juan knew that **woodworking** was a kind of carpentry. He looked up woodworking in the index at the back of the book. There were many jobs listed under woodworking. One job that caught his eye was cabinetmaking. Cabinetmaking sounded interesting to Juan.

He read about the tasks and working conditions for cabinetmakers. It sounded like cabinetmaking was what he wanted. He knew he wanted to learn more. He decided to give Fred Smith a call.

Fred told Juan to call Hans Olsen, the owner of Creative Cabinets. He gave Juan the phone number. Juan asked Fred to tell Mr. Olsen that Juan would be calling. Fred said he'd be glad to.

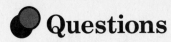 **Questions**

1. Where did Juan go to learn more about carpentry?

   _____

2. What resource did Juan use?

   _____

3. Did Juan think he might like to be a carpenter?

   _____

4. What job sounded interesting to Juan?

   _____

5. What do you think Juan should do next?

   _____

   _____

   _____

Getting Closer to a Job Decision

Juan called Hans Olsen. He explained that he was interested in learning more about cabinetmaking as a possible career. Hans seemed happy to meet with Juan. He set up a time when they could meet.

Juan went to Creative Cabinets two days later to meet with Hans. Part of their conversation is shown below.

After talking with Hans, Juan had to do a lot of thinking. He was very interested in cabinetmaking as a possible career. He knew he had to find out more. He needed more information to decide if this was the right job for him.

🖊 Questions

1. Who did Juan find to talk with about cabinetmaking?

    _____

2. One of Juan's work values is to find steady work. Does cabinetmaking seem like steady work?

    _____

3. Juan hopes to find work that is indoors. Does Hans do his work indoors?

    _____

4. By the end of the conversation, do you think Juan is still interested in cabinetmaking?

    _____

5. What do you think Juan should do next?

    _____

    _____

    _____

What This Job Is All About

People often have ideas about a job, but later they find out that the job is not what they expected.

Juan had lots of ideas about what a carpenter's job was like. After finding out about the work, he decided that he didn't really want to be a carpenter. He thought he might want to be a cabinetmaker instead. The work met his needs.

Below are important questions to answer about *any* job that interests you. Use the resources on pages 6–7 to help you find the answers. You may add your own questions as well.

Write your job interest here:

_____

(This should be Job Interest #1, if you have completed Book One.)

1. **What skills and training are needed to get this job?**
   Skills are the job skills and everyday skills needed in the job. *Training* refers to special skills that must be learned.

   _____

   _____

2. **What work experience is needed for this job?**
   Work experience is the number of years doing a certain kind of job, or types of work done that relate to a certain job.

   _____

   _____

3. **What tasks are done most often each day?**
   Tasks are the things that are done every day on the job.

   _____

   _____

4. **What are the working conditions for this job?**
   Working conditions are where and how you work. Outdoors? In a factory? In an office? Standing? Sitting?

   _____

   _____

5. **What is the usual pay range for this job?**
   Pay range refers to the starting pay and how much the pay will go up.

   _____

6. **What are the usual benefits for this job?**
   Benefits can include health, dental, and eye care; life and disability insurance; and retirement, or pension, plans.

   _____

   _____

7. **How many job openings are there in this field each year? How many will there be in five years?**
   Job openings means the number of positions waiting to be filled in this job, this year or in the future.

   _____

   _____

8. **What jobs can you advance to?**
   Advance means to move up or be promoted in the job.

   _____

   _____

9. **What is the education needed for this job?**
   A job may require a high school diploma, GED, or special certification.

   _____

   _____

10. **Is this job generally full-time or part-time?**

    _____

11. **What work schedule is usually found in this job?**
    Days? Nights? Swing shift? Weekends?

    _____

12. **Try to find someone who has this job. Is there anything about this job that the person does not like?**

    _____

    _____

• JUST FOR **FUN** •

Each word in this list can be found in the puzzle. Look across and down to find words. When you find a word, circle it in the puzzle and mark it off the list. Your teacher has the answers.

Words

ADVANCE	~~LIBRARY~~	RESOURCES
BENEFITS	PAY	SCHEDULE
EDUCATION	PART TIME	SERVICE
EMPLOYMENT	PEOPLE	WORK
FULL TIME	RELOCATE	

```
R  Q  F  L  P  R  L  G  H  E
E  D  U  C  A  T  I  O  N  M
S  Z  L  V  R  Q  B  P  S  P
O  A  L  P  T  W  R  E  E  L
U  D  T  A  T  O  A  O  R  O
R  V  I  Y  I  R  R  P  V  Y
C  A  M  B  M  K  Y  L  I  M
E  N  E  X  E  N  G  E  C  E
S  C  H  E  D  U  L  E  E  N
R  E  L  O  C  A  T  E  P  T
F  B  E  N  E  F  I  T  S  Z
```

Write a sentence using two or three words from the list above. <u>Underline</u> the words from the list.

Example: I am looking for <u>part-time</u> <u>employment</u> in the <u>library</u>.

_____

_____

_____

Barriers

When something stands in your way, it is called a **barrier**. Sometimes, barriers can make it hard for you to get the job you want.

There may be a barrier between your needs and what a job requires. For example, your job interest may not be available in your area. Are you willing to move? If not, you may need to look into a different job.

Often, you can overcome barriers. If you do not have enough training for a job, that is a barrier. To overcome this barrier, you may decide to go back to school to get the training you need.

Low starting pay may be a barrier. Pay rate usually goes up with experience. You may decide to take a job with low pay to gain experience. You would have to cut expenses for a while. When you make decisions like this, you are overcoming your barriers.

You need to think about your job choice. Find out if it meets your needs. You may find there are barriers. You will need to decide whether you can overcome these barriers. The next activity will help you do this.

Is This the Job for You?

Now you will compare what you *want* out of a job with what you *know* about your job interest.

Directions

Step 1. Look at your answers on pages 4–5, What I Want in a Job. Pay attention to the ones you circled as most important.

Step 2. Look at pages 14–15, What This Job Is All About.

Step 3. Read the questions below. Put a check under YES, NO, or NOT SURE to best show how your wants match up with what you know about the job.

Questions About Your Job Interest

	YES	NO	NOT SURE
1. Do you now have the skills and training needed?	☐	☐	☐
2. Do you have the work experience needed?	☐	☐	☐
3. Do you like to do the kind of tasks this job requires?	☐	☐	☐
4. Are the working conditions what you want?	☐	☐	☐
5. Does the starting pay meet your needs?	☐	☐	☐
6. Are the benefits what you want?	☐	☐	☐
7. Are there many openings for this job?	☐	☐	☐
8. Are there chances to be promoted?	☐	☐	☐
9. Do you have the education needed?	☐	☐	☐
10. Can you work the schedule you want?	☐	☐	☐

Right now, are you still interested in this job? Use the space below to write why or why not.

_____

_____

_____

Step 4. Look back at your answers on page 18. If you have:

- **nearly all** NO answers, this is probably **not** the best job for you. You may need to repeat this unit, using a different job choice. It might be helpful to go back to Book One and find another job interest. Ask your teacher to help you decide.

- **several** NOT SURE answers, you need to learn more about the job. Go back to your resources until you can answer YES or NO.

- **a few** NO answers, there may be problems or barriers with this job. You may find ways to overcome some of these NO barriers.

Step 5. In the spaces below, write in any three questions that you answered with NO. Then, write how you think you can overcome each barrier.

NO answer #1:

_____

How can you overcome this barrier?

_____

_____

NO answer #2:

_____

How can you overcome this barrier?

_____

_____

NO answer #3:

_____

How can you overcome this barrier?

_____

_____

It is a good idea to do this with all of your NO answers.

Putting It All Together

You have learned how to get good information about jobs. You have

- looked at what you want from a job,

- found out what one job is really like,

- decided if this job choice gives you what you want and need in a job, and

- looked at any barriers that you might have to overcome.

These steps will help you find the job that is right for you. Use these steps to find out about *any* job you are interested in. This information can help you now, as well as in the future.

Look at the picture below. At one end of the highway, write your name or draw a picture of yourself. At the other end, write the name of the job you want. Then, use the signs along the road to tell how you might overcome your barriers. Add as many signs as you wish.

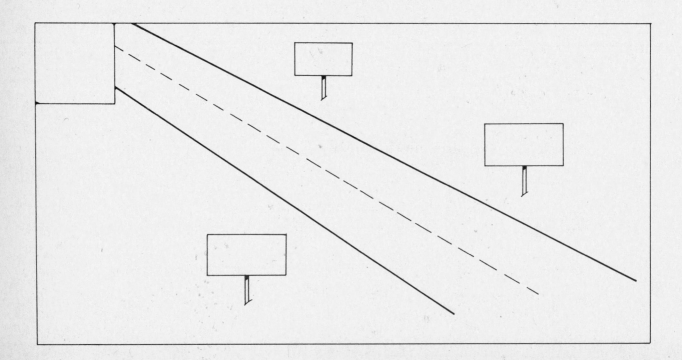

JOB OPENINGS
UNIT TWO

 # Finding Available Jobs

In Unit One, you learned how to find and use good information about your job choice. You decided if it was the right work for you. In this unit, you will learn how to find job openings. These are positions that are waiting to be filled. There may be more ways to find job openings than you might think.

How This Unit Will Help You

Knowing how and where to find a job is important. With good information, you will be more likely to find the job that is right for you.

In this unit you will

- learn how to get **job information**

- build a **network**

- learn how to find **job openings**

- decide which jobs you want to **apply** for

Juan's Story

Juan García was ready to find a job opening. He went back to the employment service. He met with Ms. Cook, the job counselor he had talked with before. Juan told her how excited he was about becoming a cabinetmaker. He thought that this job was just right. He would make a good living for himself and his family.

Ms. Cook told Juan that his next step was to find job openings for a cabinetmaker's helper. She told him there were many ways to find these openings. The employment service was a good place to start. There were usually a few jobs of this type listed there.

Ms. Cook told Juan that more than one-half of the jobs available are found through **networking**. Networking, she said, was building up a list of people who might help him find openings. Juan's family, friends, classmates, co-workers, former employers, and teachers could form his network. These people may not know of job openings, but they may know someone who does. That is how a network develops.

Another way to find openings, Ms. Cook said, is to contact employers directly. For Juan, this would mean calling all the cabinet shops in the area, as he had done with Creative Cabinets.

Ms. Cook also mentioned the want ads in the local newspaper. Here, employers advertise jobs that are open.

● Questions About the Story

1. What are three ways to find job openings?

   _____

   _____

   _____

2. What works the best for more than one-half of the people looking for work?

   _____

3. Who can be part of someone's network?

   _____

   _____

   _____

4. Where are jobs advertised?

   _____

5. Does the employment service have lists of job openings?

   _____

Answers

1. networking, contacting employers directly, want ads, or employment service 2. networking 3. family, friends, classmates, co-workers, former employers, teachers 4. want ads 5. yes

Your Network

Some of your most important resources are the people you know. These people make up your **network**. A network is a group of many people who are all connected. You may think that your network is made up only of people who are close to you. People like family, friends, co-workers, and other students are just a start. Each of these people knows many others. They have bosses, co-workers, and friends who may know about job openings.

If you know two people, who each know two others, and those people also each know two others . . .

Your network can grow fast. It helps to have a simple way to keep track of your contacts. One way is to use **network cards**. A sample is shown here.

Who to contact _____	
What company _____	
Phone number _____	
Referred by _____	
After the contact:	
What to do next _____	
_____	

Network cards help you keep track of important details about your contacts. Use the back side of the card for any other information about the contact.

You can buy 3″ × 5″ cards to use for your network cards. If you prefer, you can write the information in a notebook.

Using a Network Card

Linda is looking for a job as a landscaper. She knows all about the work, and she has the skills needed for the job. Linda knows that landscaping is done in parks, at colleges, and at large companies.

Linda is ready to look for job openings. She wants to give networking a try. She decides to call her cousin Jim first. He knows many people, and Linda thinks he might be able to help her. Here is part of their conversation:

"Hi, Jim, this is Linda. I am looking for a job as a landscaper. Do you know where there might be any job openings?"

"Hi, Linda. I don't know of any job openings, but you might try my friend Bill Thomas. He is the groundskeeper at Hi-Tek. His number is 555-1234. Tell him I told you to call."

After talking with Jim, Linda knew what to do next. She filled out the bottom section of her network card for Jim.

Who to contact ___Jim_____

What company _____

Phone number ___555-3402_____

Referred by ___me_____

After the contact:

What to do next ___Call Bill Thomas_____555-1234___
___Fill out network card for Bill_____

Linda is now ready to fill out a new network card.

Fill in the next three lines of Linda's new network card for Bill.

Who to contact	*Bill Thomas*
What company	
Phone number	
Referred by	
After the contact:	
What to do next	

Here is part of the call that Linda made next:

"Hello, Mr. Thomas, my name is Linda Stevens. Jim Evans suggested I call you. I am looking for a landscaping job. Do you know of any openings?"

"I'm not sure, but I think the community college is hiring. Tom Chan is in charge of the grounds there. Give him a call. You can tell him I sent you."

Go back up to Linda's network card for Bill. Fill in *What to do next*.

Linda is building a network. This is what her network looks like:

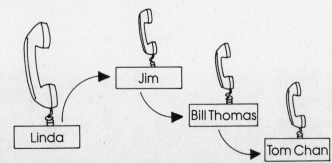

Start Your Network

You can make as many network cards as you want. When you look for a new job, the network you build will serve you well.

What is your job interest?

_____

Think of someone who might be a good contact for you. This person might know of a job opening for this type of work. Or, if this person does not know about an opening, he or she may know someone else who does.

Directions
Step 1. Fill in this network card with the name of your contact person.

```
┌─────────────────────────────────────────────────┐
│                                                   │
│  Who to contact _____  │
│  What company _____  │
│  Phone number _____  │
│  Referred by _____  │
│  After the contact:                               │
│  What to do next _____  │
│  _____ │
│                                                   │
└─────────────────────────────────────────────────┘
```

Step 2. Think about what you want to ask your contact person. Give this person a call.

Step 3. Fill in *What to do next* after the call.

Remember: Buy a package of 3″ × 5″ cards to use for your network cards. It will be worth the price. If you prefer, use a notebook.

Put any extra information on the back of the card.

Contacting Employers Directly

Another kind of network is a list of possible employers. You can make a list of all the employers in your area who may have the kind of job opening you are looking for. The names, addresses, and phone numbers of these employers are in the yellow pages of the phone book.

Juan García was ready to learn more about cabinetmaking openings in his area. He looked in the yellow pages. He found the heading *Cabinets & Cabinetmakers*.

He needed to start by calling one shop to ask if they had openings, or knew of any other shop that did. He was building a network of employers.

Here is the part of the yellow pages where Juan found what he needed:

Butter	
HART CREAMERY INC	
14048 N Spruce	555-0290

Buttons	
Buttons Unlimited	
22 S King	555-4451

Cabinets & Cabinetmakers	
BUILT RIGHT CABINETS	
3408 N Cedar	555-0233
Cabinets Unlimited	
13422 S River Rd	555-3763
CREATIVE CABINETS	
542 S Center..................	555-5099
Custom Cabinets	
1858 N Broadway	555-1688

Cable Splicing	
Acme Splicing	
1008 42nd Ave NW	555-8204
ST. JOHN COMMUNICATIONS	
222 G Street	555-5032

Fill in the missing information below.

Name: *Built Right Cabinets*

Address: _____

Phone: _____

Juan will later fill out network cards for all four cabinetmakers.

An Important Call

Juan was a little nervous about making his first call, but he knew he could do it. He had a pencil, paper, and calendar ready. He made sure the room was quiet when he placed the call. Here is the conversation that took place:

man: Good morning, Built Right Cabinets.

Juan: Good morning, this is Juan García. I would like to talk to the personnel department, please.

man: Just a moment, I'll connect you.

Anita: This is Anita Miller. How can I help you?

Juan: Hello, my name is Juan García. I am interested in finding work as a cabinetmaker's helper. Do you have any openings at your shop?

Anita: I'm sorry, Juan. We don't have any openings right now. Things may pick up in a few weeks. Give me a call then, and I'll see what I can do.

Juan: Thank you for your time. I will call you back in two weeks.

After the call, Juan filled out a network card for this contact. He wrote down Anita Miller's name right away so that he would not forget it.

Who to contact _Anita Miller_____

What company _____

Phone number _____

Referred by _____

After the contact:

What to do next _____

_____

Fill out the rest of the card as Juan would. Be sure to include the date to call back.

Juan put the card in a special place where he would be sure to see it. What do you think Juan should do next?

_____

Using the Want Ads

Your local newspaper is an important source of information on job openings. Most newspapers have a classified advertising section. This section includes "want ads"—often called "help wanted," "positions open," or "jobs." Whatever they are called, these ads can help you find out about a job.

Want ads are organized alphabetically, by the first letter of the job title or first word in the ad. An ad for an auto mechanic would come before that of a baker's assistant, because *a* comes before *b* in the alphabet.

If the ad for an auto mechanic started with the word *mechanic*, then where would it be? It would be under the letter *m*, for mechanic. So you may have to look under more than one letter to find the job you are looking for. You may have to know several ways the same job can be listed.

Abbreviations: Employers use abbreviations, or short forms of a word, to get across their ideas in want ads. These short forms of words can often be confusing. Here is a list of commonly used abbreviations.

Abbreviation	Meaning	Abbreviation	Meaning
appt.	appointment	mech.	mechanical(ly)
assist.	assistant	min.	minimum
avail.	available	M–F	Monday through Friday
bens.	benefits		
co.	company	mo., mos.	month, months
comm.	commission	pd.	paid
cond., conds.	condition, conditions	pers.	person
dip.	diploma	pref.	preferred
disc.	discount	PT, pt	part-time
drvs.	drivers	ref.	references
EOE.	equal opportunity employer	req.	required
		sal.	salary
exc., exce., or excel.	excellent	sec'y	secretary
exp., exper.	experience(d)	tel.	telephone
FT, ft	full-time	vac., vacs.	vacation(s)
hol., holi.	holidays	w/	with
hr.	hour	wk.	week
HS, hs	high school	wkg.	working
immed.	immediate(ly)	wpm	words per minute (typing)
lics.	license		
		yr., yrs.	year, years

 # Want Ad Practice

Look at this want ad.

> DIETARY ASSISTANT, FT, exc. pay, bens. & wkg. conds. Apply in pers. M–F 10–2, Elder Hostel, 1916 Pierce St. EOE

When the abbreviations are written out in full, the ad would read like this:

> DIETARY ASSISTANT, Full-time, excellent pay, benefits, and working conditions. Apply in person, Monday through Friday from 10 A.M. to 2 P.M. at Elder Hostel, 1916 Pierce Street. Equal Opportunity Employer.

Directions
Step 1.
In your local paper, find one want ad for a job that interests you. Copy it, or cut it out and paste it, in the space.

Step 2.
Now rewrite the ad. Replace all abbreviations with the words they stand for.

_____

_____

_____

_____

_____

Choose a Job for Juan

Below you will see Juan García, surrounded by samples of want ads.

Directions
Step 1. Draw a line from Juan to the want ads that you think he may be interested in.

Step 2. Circle the one job opening that you think is **best** for Juan.

Step 3. Use the space at the bottom of the page to tell why you think that job is best for Juan.

CABINETMAKERS: Career opportunity for exp. & entry level cabinet-makers. Call Samuel 555-0999 (8 A.M.–3 P.M.)

CABINETMAKER: Union shop, exp only. Full medical benefits. Apply at 104 E Lake, Carmel

PARTS Driver: good driving record, FT position. Apply in person: 432 Bond St, Davis

CABINET SHOP — custom — min 2 yrs experience 555-3718

CABLE TV — exp. underground personnel needed for immediate openings. 555-0386

MECHANIC: small engines, exper. necessary. Fullerton 555-0728

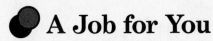 **A Job for You**

What is your job interest from Unit One?

_____

Directions

Step 1. In the box below, write your name or draw a picture of yourself.

Step 2. Look in your local paper for some want ads for your job interest. If you do not find your job listed, look for similar ones that might interest you.

Step 3. Copy the ads, or cut them out and paste them, around "you" below.

Step 4. Circle the one ad that seems **best** for you.

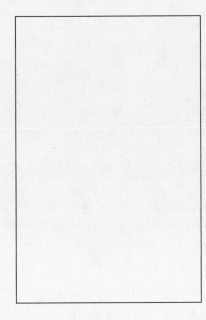

Learning About Job Openings

You have worked hard to find out about openings for your job interest. You started your network, and you learned about calling employers. You also learned how to read want ads.

Which of these ways of finding openings do you think will work best for you? Use the space below to write a few sentences about how you feel. If you prefer, you can draw a picture to show your feelings.

GETTING READY
UNIT THREE

Preparing to Apply

In this unit, you will put together information about yourself. You will need this information to apply for a job.

First, you will complete your **personal history**. Your personal history tells about your working life—what you know and where you learned it.

Next, you will write a **resume**. A resume is a short summary of your personal history. It will sell your special skills and qualities to a new employer. You will also learn to write **cover letters** to send with your resume.

How This Unit Will Help You

This unit will help you look at your skills and your strengths. You will put this information in writing. This will make applying for jobs much easier for you.

In this unit you will

- write your **personal history**

- decide which of your **skills** best describe you

- write a **resume**

- write a **cover letter**

Your Personal History

You have been successful in many areas of your life. Look closely at yourself. You will find you have valuable skills and strengths. Your skills and strengths make up your personal history.

First, you will think about skills you learned in school. Next, you will look at skills learned from on-the-job experience. Then, you will look at skills gained from unpaid work, and skills learned from being a family member. Finally, you will think about your strengths.

Education

Employers want to know about your education. Think about your classes and any other activities. Answer the following questions:

What school did you attend last?

_____

What skills did you learn?

_____

_____

Which skills that you learned at school did you like the best?

_____

_____

Work History

If you have held a paying job, fill in this section. If not,
go on to the next page.

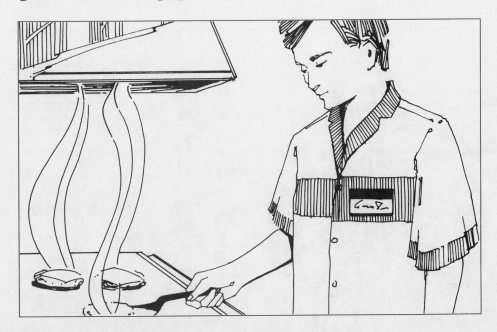

Fill out the following about your most recent job:

Name of Employer _____

Job Title _____ Dates: from _____ to _____

What are you most proud of about this job?

_____

What skills did you use?

_____

Do the same with your next most recent job:

Name of Employer _____

Job Title _____ Dates: from _____ to _____

What are you most proud of about this job?

_____

What skills did you use?

_____

You may wish to think about other jobs you have had. Use
a separate sheet of paper. Write about your successes.

Military Experience

The military is another source of on-the-job learning. If you have military experience, fill in this section. If not, go on to the next page.

Name of Service Branch _____

Dates: from _____ to _____

Job Title _____

What special training did you get?

_____

Did you earn any certificates, special awards, or recognition?

_____

_____

What skills did you use?

_____

_____

_____

Now you have completed your *paid* work history.

Mary's Story

Mary was surprised at how much she had learned about herself. Her New Jobs class was exciting. She found out she really did have a lot of skills.

At first it was frightening when her husband left. She was stunned. She had never worked before. She had two children, no job, and no money. She spent the first two weeks crying.

Mary went on public aid. She was glad to have help, but wanted to get a job to support herself and her family.

Her caseworker told her about the New Jobs Program. Mary joined the class eagerly. In the class, she learned that she was not alone. Many others shared her sense of helplessness. They, too, felt they had no job skills to offer.

After a short time in class, Mary learned that she had many job skills. She had been a volunteer teacher at her church for years. She had also raised money to help the homeless. These activities had taken skill and patience.

Mary felt better about her ability to find a job. Even though she had never held a job, she had many skills that employers would like.

🔵 Questions About the Story

1. Where did Mary get most of her experience?

_____

_____

2. What do you think employers will like about Mary?

_____

_____

🔵 Volunteer Work

As adults, we often do unpaid work. This is called
volunteer work. Sometimes, it is for family reasons. For
example, you may coach your child's softball team. Other
times, it is to help others. You may volunteer to help the
Red Cross. Though not paid, these activities are still
work. As a volunteer, you use many skills. You often learn
new things, too. These skills are important to employers.

Have you ever done volunteer work? What did you do?

_____

_____

_____

What skills did you use?

_____

_____

_____

Put a check by the skills that will help you with the job
that interests you.

Answers

1. from family life and volunteer work 2. answers will vary

Family and Free Time

Family life is another area where you use many skills. You may not think these skills have much to do with work. But family life and work skills are very closely connected. Cooking, cleaning, and taking care of children all require skills that employers want.

You may do things in your family or free time that require many skills. A woman may plan her family budget. She uses good math skills. A man who collects stamps may be skilled in detail work. Other skills may include organization, creativity, or working with others.

In the space below, list some activities that you do in your family life and in your free time.

_____

_____

_____

Can you think of the skills that you use to do these activities?

_____

_____

_____

What Are Your Strengths?

In addition to skills, you have **strengths** that are important to an employer. Strengths are personal qualities, such as being honest or coming to work on time. You need to let employers know what your strengths are.

For each of the following strengths, put a check under USUALLY, SOMETIMES, or RARELY to show how often you use that strength. For example, if you are very dependable, put a check under USUALLY.

I am:	USUALLY	SOMETIMES	RARELY
dependable	☐	☐	☐
hardworking	☐	☐	☐
a good listener	☐	☐	☐
helpful to others	☐	☐	☐
on time	☐	☐	☐
honest	☐	☐	☐
friendly	☐	☐	☐
a good learner	☐	☐	☐
organized	☐	☐	☐
understanding of others	☐	☐	☐
flexible	☐	☐	☐
enthusiastic	☐	☐	☐
patient	☐	☐	☐
eager to get ahead	☐	☐	☐
able to follow directions	☐	☐	☐
proud of my work	☐	☐	☐
neat in appearance	☐	☐	☐

Look over your USUALLY column.

These are your strengths. Decide which ones best stand for you as a worker. Write your five best strengths below.

1. _____

2. _____

3. _____

4. _____

5. _____

Write two or three sentences about yourself as a worker. Try to use all five strengths that you listed.

_____

_____

_____

_____

 # Starting Your Resume

You have collected your personal history. Now it is time to write a **resume**. A resume is a brief summary of your strengths and experience. You may need a resume to apply for some jobs.

There are many ways to write a resume. You will write a resume that shows your strengths. A resume is usually one page long, and it is *always* typed.

Directions
Fill out all of the parts of this resume. Later, you will decide on the order that you would like to use to present your information.

Heading: This comes at the top of the page. It includes your name, address, and phone number. The phone number is very important. Be sure that you will get the message if an employer calls.

Experience: This tells about the job skills you have from work, military, volunteer, family, or free-time experience. You may want to look back to pages 37–41.

Begin with your most recent job, paid or unpaid. List all of the skills that you used on this job.

Tell how much time you spent there. (Example: I worked three years as a volunteer for . . .)

Then, list your next most recent job, paid or unpaid. List some different skills if you can.

name
address
phone

Experience

Strengths: You will find your strengths on page 43. This section is your chance to tell about your good work habits.

Training: You wrote your educational history on page 36. You will rewrite it here. Think about the type of work you want to do. Show the skills you have been trained for that you would use at this job. Start with your most recent training. List any special certification you have earned.

References: References are people who are willing to say good things about you and can verify facts in your resume. A good reference might be someone you have done work for. Do not use family members.

Before you use people as references, first ask them if you can use their names. Be sure they will say good things about you!

List the name, address, and phone number for at least three references.

Strengths

Training

References

Sample Resume

Jolyn Walkingstar
1234 N. Howard Street
Portland, Oregon 97022
(503) 555-1071

STRENGTHS: I am hardworking and always on time. I am friendly and work well with others. I follow directions well. I have enthusiasm, and I enjoy meeting new people. I am very well organized and am flexible in organizing my work. I take pride in what I do.

EXPERIENCE: I have four years of volunteer experience at my children's school. I organized and managed a parent support group. I called regular meetings, set the agenda, sent out notices, and answered questions. I also worked with the school administration and teachers. In three years, I got enough money to add more than 500 books to the library.

I have two years of experience as a waitress at Cook and Shake Deli. I took orders, handled money, and dealt with the public.

REFERENCES: Sondra Brown, Principal
James Audubon Elementary School
204 Thompson St.
Portland, OR 97013
(503) 555-2919

Nancy Walker, President
Parent Teachers Association
James Audubon Elementary School
204 Thompson St.
Portland, OR 97013
(503) 555-2919

D. J. Johnston
Cook and Shake Deli
8650 N. Broadway
Portland, OR 97022
(503) 555-7406

🔴 Questions

Jolyn wanted her resume to show her strengths.

1. Why do you think Jolyn left *training* off her resume?

_____

_____

_____

2. Jolyn wrote about her unpaid experience. What skills did she highlight?

_____

_____

_____

Some employers will want to see your resume. Others will not. If you use one, remember that

- a final resume is always typed

- a resume has no errors in spelling, punctuation, or grammar

- a resume is typed on good-quality paper

A resume should be kept up-to-date. Be sure to include your most recent experiences on your resume.

In the next activity, you will write a practice resume.

Answers

1. because she probably felt that her training was weaker than her strengths and experience   2. organizing, managing, planning, communicating, problem-solving, and fund-raising skills

Your Resume

The Heading of your resume is always at the top of the page. It includes your name, address, and phone number. Your References always come last.

The other three parts of a resume are Experience, Strengths, and Training. They should go in the order that best fits you.

For example, if you feel that your Experience section is the best, it should come first. If you have had little experience, then you might start with the Strengths or the Training section.

Now you will decide how you want to organize your resume.

Directions

Step 1. Go to pages 44 and 45. Decide which section is your best. Mark that section #1.

Step 2. Decide which section is your second best. Mark that section #2.

Step 3. Look at your training. If you think this section is weak, you may leave it out, or put it just before your references.

On the next page, write out the titles of your three best sections. Put them in the order you decided to use. Then, copy the information from pages 44 and 45.

Finally, check what you wrote. Is everything correct? If so, write the information again on a separate sheet of paper. The final copy of your resume should be typed.

_____
Name

_____
Street Address

_____
City, State, Zip

_____
Phone Number

1 _____:

2 _____:

3 _____ (if used):

References:

Yvette's Cover Letter

When you answer a want ad about a job, you will send your resume. You also need to write a **cover letter** to send with it. The cover letter tells the employer what job you are applying for. It needs to be typed with no errors.

In her Sunday paper, Yvette Hart saw this ad:

> Receptionist in busy law office. Good phone skills, must like people. Exp pref. Good bens, salary, work conds. Send resume to Sara White, Legal Aid Society, PO Box 501, New York, NY 10020

Yvette wrote this cover letter to send with her resume:

Return Address: Put your address and the date here.

Inside Address: Put the name of the person, company, and address here.

Greeting: Put the name of the person you are writing to here. If you do not know the person's name, write "Dear Sir or Madam."

Opening: In the first paragraph, put the name of the job. Also tell where you read or heard about the job.

Strengths: List your skills and experience that fit this job.

Closing: Tell how you can be reached. Be sure to leave a three-line space for your signature, then type your name below.

3929 East 45th St.
New York, NY 10020
October 9, 199__

Ms. Sara White
Legal Aid Society
PO Box 501
New York, NY 10020

Dear Ms. White:

I am sending my resume to apply for the position of receptionist that you advertised in the New York Times. I am sure that I have the skills needed for the job.

I like meeting new people, I enjoy using the phone, and I have telephone experience from a volunteer position. I also have worked with a variety of people, and I am used to dealing with many different bosses.

I can be reached at 555-6979. I look forward to hearing from you.

Sincerely,

Yvette Hart

Yvette Hart

 # Writing Your Cover Letter

Directions

Step 1. Find a want ad that you wish to respond to. Copy it, or cut it out and paste it, in the space below. If you prefer, use the one below.

Step 2. Write a cover letter to answer your ad.

Parts Clerk: FT, stable work history req. Good phone and writing skills. Must like people. Good pay and bens. Paid vacs. Resume to: Acme Auto Parts, 1731 S. River Ave., Rose, CA 95678

_____

_____

_____

_____

_____

_____

_____

Dear _____ :

_____

_____

_____

_____

Sincerely,

_____

What Have You Learned?

You have learned a lot about your strengths and skills. Were there any surprises for you? Write how you feel about using these strengths and skills in the future.

Applying for a Job

In Unit Three, you looked at the skills that make you a good worker. Now you are ready to **apply** for a job. In this unit, you will learn how to fill out applications. Your personal history and resume will help you. You will also need to gather more information. You will need to give dates and places for your education, your work, and your volunteer experience.

How This Unit Will Help You

The job application is one of the most important forms you will ever fill out. If the application is neat and complete, you stand a very good chance of getting an interview. If you get an interview, you have a good chance of getting the job.

In this unit you will

• prepare a **practice application**

• fill out a real **job application**

Filling Out Your Practice Application

In this unit, you will fill out two job applications: a **practice application** and a real job application. When you have filled out the practice application, you can tear it out of the book. Then, you can take it with you to help you fill out other job applications.

Because the practice application is *practice*, you will fill it out in *pencil*. You should use a pen to fill out all other applications. Here are some more tips for filling out your practice application:

- Read over the application before writing anything.

- Use a pencil so you can correct mistakes.

- Print with your neatest handwriting (use ALL CAPITALS).

- Use a dictionary for correct spelling.

- Do NOT skip any sections. Write NA if the section does not apply to you.

- Do NOT cross out any words. Erase and correct any mistakes.

- Have someone who is good at spelling check your work.

Following Directions

When you fill out a job application, you must follow the directions carefully.

Directions

Step 1. Look over the list of practice application tips on page 54.

Step 2. Answer the questions below. Circle T for true and F for false.

When you fill out your **practice** application:

1. T   F   Read over the application before you write anything.

2. T   F   Use your neatest printing.

3. T   F   Write with a pen.

4. T   F   Cross out words if you make a mistake.

5. T   F   Write with all capital letters.

6. T   F   Skip sections if you want to.

The person shown here used the tips for the practice application to fill out a **real** job application.

Remember: Always read over the application and follow the directions before writing anything.

Answers

1. T 2. T 3. F 4. F 5. T 6. F

 # Practice Application

Now you are ready to fill out a practice application. Be as complete as you can.

Directions
Use a pencil. Print in ALL CAPITALS. Write NA if the section does not apply to you.

Personal Information
Along with your name and address, this section asks for the date. That means today's date. You need to know your social security number. If you are a citizen of the United States, check YES. If you are not a U.S. citizen, be sure you have your alien registration number.

Job Interest
List the title of the position you want to apply for. Applications often ask what salary you expect. Unless you know the exact salary of the job you are applying for, just write OPEN. If you want this job right away, write NOW by "date available."

Education
List information about where you went to school. If you went to high school, tell where and when you last attended. If you completed the GED, list it in the place for high school. The last item in this section is Other Special Knowledge or Skills. This is your chance to list the skills that you wrote on page 36.

Work History
List your most recent job first. The application asks for the dates you worked there (example: 3/1/88 to 9/9/91). You need to know the employer's name and address. Briefly tell about your job title and duties. List your supervisor's name. Tell why you left this job (if you were fired, write TERMINATED). Tell how much you earned.

Repeat these steps for the job you had before this one. List up to four jobs.

PRACTICE APPLICATION Please use a pencil and PRINT the entire application.

Personal Information		
PRINT NAME	DATE	
(Last) (First) (Middle)	SOCIAL SECURITY #	
ADDRESS		
(Number and Street)	TELEPHONE	
(City) (State) (Zip Code)		
☐ YES CITIZEN OF THE U.S.? ☐ NO *If NO, are you legally allowed to work in the U.S.?	☐ YES Write registration ☐ NO number here	

Job Interest		
POSITION DESIRED	SALARY EXPECTED	DATE AVAILABLE

Education

	SCHOOL NAME	ADDRESS	MAJOR STUDIES	DEGREE(S)	DATES ATTENDED
HIGH SCHOOL					
COLLEGE					
BUSINESS or VOCATIONAL					

OTHER SPECIAL KNOWLEDGE OR SKILLS

Work History

List all employment, starting with your most recent employer. Include job-related volunteer work.

DATES OF EMPLOYMENT	EMPLOYER NAME AND ADDRESS	JOB TITLE AND DUTIES	NAME OF SUPERVISOR	REASON FOR LEAVING	HIGHEST SALARY

Military				
BRANCH OF U.S. SERVICE	DATE ENTERED	DATE DISCHARGED	FINAL RANK	TYPE DISCHARGE

Office Skills		
Do you type? ☐ YES ☐ NO	*If YES, WPM _____	WHAT OFFICE MACHINES CAN YOU OPERATE?

Other Information
HAVE YOU EVER BEEN CONVICTED OF A FELONY? ☐ YES ☐ NO   *If YES, please explain

Personal References

List the names and phone numbers of three references. No relatives please.

NAME	ADDRESS	PHONE

I swear all statements in this application are true and correct. I understand that any false answers will be cause for dismissal if I am hired. I give permission for the investigation of all statements in this application. This includes contacting former employers.

Applicant Signature _____

— — — — — — — — — — — — — — — — — — fold line A — — — — — — — — — — — — — — — — —

List your **strengths**.

_____

_____

_____

_____

_____

fold line B

This practice application belongs to:

_____

your name

- Use ink on a real application.
- Print neatly.
- Fill out **all** sections.
- Write **NA** if something doesn't apply to you.

Military

If you have no military experience, print NA in the box that says "Branch of U.S. Service." If you were in the military, fill out all five boxes.

Office Skills

If you know how to type, check YES. Write how many words per minute you can type. You may be asked about office machines. Some examples are copy machines, computers, adding machines, and phones.

Other Information

If you have not been convicted of a felony, check NO. If the answer is YES, do **not** put a check. Instead, write WOULD LIKE TO DISCUSS. If you do this, be prepared to talk about it. Try to think of something positive from the experience. Perhaps you learned something valuable. There are employers who will like you for your honesty. Do not tell lies about your past. Once the truth is found out, the company has the right to fire you for lying.

WOULD LIKE TO DISCUSS is a good answer for any question that is too difficult for a short answer.

Personal References

You need to list three references. Choose people who can tell about your good work habits. Do not list relatives.

Your Signature

This is where you sign your name. Use your regular signature; do not print. By signing, you are saying that you have been truthful.

Using Your Practice Application

If you wish to take your practice application out of the book:

Step 1. Cut or tear it out of the book.

Step 2. Fold it in half along fold line A.

Step 3. Fold it in half again, along fold line B.

Write your name on the front. On the back, list the strengths you wrote on page 43.

A Real Application

Now you have the chance to fill out a real company's application. You can use the information from your practice application.

Directions
Fill in the Marriott application on pages 61–62. Take your time. For this and all real applications, use *ink*. Remember to print in ALL CAPITALS.

Application Tips

Personal Data
Permanent Address: If your home address is permanent, write SAME. If you move a lot, use the address of a friend or relative who will not move often.

Employment Information
Position(s) applied for: Write the job title of the job you are applying for.

Previously employed by Marriott: Write NA if you have never worked at Marriott, or have never applied for work there.

How referred to Marriott: Write how you heard about the job.

Work shifts: You can choose which shifts you are willing to work. However, marking one choice may limit your chances of getting hired.

Type of employment: Mark whether you want full-time or part-time work.

Education and Training
Foreign languages: If you speak a language other than English, be sure to tell the employer.

Food and Beverage Areas
If you want to work serving food or drinks, you may need to answer questions about diseases. Some states, listed on the bottom of page 62, do not allow these questions to be asked. If you live in a state where the questions may not be asked, leave this section blank.

Marriott
HOTELS · RESORTS · SUITES

AN EQUAL OPPORTUNITY / AFFIRMATIVE ACTION EMPLOYER*

Application for Employment

PERSONAL DATA

LAST NAME   FIRST   MIDDLE INITIAL

HOME ADDRESS	PERMANENT ADDRESS
Street	Street
City State Zip	City State Zip
Telephone - Area Code Number ( )	Telephone - Area Code Number ( )

EMPLOYMENT INFORMATION

Position(s) applied for   Salary Desired

$ per hour

PLEASE INITIAL   *I understand that an offer of employment, and my continued employment with Marriott are contingent upon satisfactory proof of my authorization to work in the United States.*

SOCIAL SECURITY NUMBER   Are you 18 years of age or over? ☐ Yes ☐ No

If you are a veteran of any branch of the U.S. Armed Forces, did you acquire skills which would be relevant for the position for which you are applying? ☐ Yes ☐ No   If yes, please describe:

Have you ever been employed by ☐ or previously applied for ☐ a position with Marriott or any of its subsidiaries?
If so, please check appropriate space above and specify location(s) and date(s).

How were you referred to Marriott?

Marriott invites applicants to **voluntarily** disclose any disability for purposes of assisting the company in it's affirmative action efforts. If you are a qualified individual with a disability and would like to be considered under Marriott's Affirmative Action Program, please inform us.

The following conditions may be required at some point in a job assignment. If required, would you be willing to work:

a) Shift Work? ☐ Yes ☐ No b) Rotational work schedule? ☐ Yes ☐ No

c) Work schedule other than Monday thru Friday? ☐ Yes ☐ No d) Overtime? ☐ Yes ☐ No

When could you be available to begin work:

Type of employment desired: ☐ Full-time ☐ Part-time ☐ Temporary ☐ Summer ☐ Cooperative Education

EDUCATION AND TRAINING

Type of School	Name & Address of School	Graduated Yes	Graduated No	Type of Degree Diploma or Certificate	Major/Minor Field of Study
High School	Dates Attended				
College or University					
Other Education					

FOREIGN LANGUAGES   1. _____   ☐ READ   ☐ WRITE   ☐ SPEAK
(List fluent only)   2. _____   ☐ READ   ☐ WRITE   ☐ SPEAK

81007 6/89

TO BE COMPLETED ONLY BY INDIVIDUALS APPLYING FOR POSITIONS IN FOOD AND BEVERAGE AREAS *
* THIS INQUIRY MAY BE PROHIBITED IN CERTAIN STATES. SEE REVERSE SIDE.

Do you now have or have you had within the last six months:

	Yes*	No		Yes*	No
Any gastro-intestinal infections?	___	___	Typhoid	___	___
Salmonella	___	___	Hepatitis A	___	___
Dysentery	___	___	print name date		

*If the answer is "yes", you will not necessarily be barred from employment; however, you must obtain medical certification that you are free from the above stated condition(s) before you can be employed for positions in the Food and Beverage Areas.

Reprinted courtesy of Marriott Corporation.

Have you been convicted of a felony within the last five years? ☐ Yes ☐ No

If yes, please briefly describe the circumstances of your conviction, indicating the date, nature, and place of the offense and disposition of the case.

_____

_____

_____

_____

EMPLOYMENT EXPERIENCE

Please list your job history for the past five years* (or last three employers). Start with your present status and note any periods in which you were not employed. Include U.S. military service, previous Marriott experience, summer/part-time jobs, and cooperative education assignments.

Company Name and Address	Dates Employed Month Year	Base Rate of Pay	Position Title and Description of Duties	Reason for Leaving
_____ Telephone ( )	From _____ To _____	Starting $ ____ Per Final $ ____ Per		Supervisor
_____ Telephone ( )	From _____ To _____	Starting $ ____ Per Final $ ____ Per		Supervisor
_____ Telephone ( )	From _____ To _____	Starting $ ____ Per Final $ ____ Per		Supervisor

Do you have any objections to our contacting your present employer to verify the above?

☐ No, you may contact anytime. ☐ Do not contact now, you may contact at a later date. (Please specify e.g., after acceptance of offer or a specific date, if appropriate.)

PLEASE READ THE FOLLOWING STATEMENTS CAREFULLY

1. I authorize the persons, schools, current employer (if approved by me in the Employment Experience Section) and other organizations or employers named in this application to provide Marriott with any relevant information that may be required to arrive at an employment decision.
2. I understand and agree that:
   a) The information that I have provided is accurate to the best of my knowledge and subject to verification by Marriott.
   b) A material misrepresentation or deliberate omission of a fact in my application may be justification for refusal of employment or, if employed, termination by Marriott.
   3) Although management makes every effort to accommodate individual preferences, business needs at times make the following conditions mandatory: overtime, shift work, a rotating work schedule, or a work schedule other than Monday through Friday. I understand and accept these conditions of my continuing employment.
3. I understand that nothing contained in this employment application or in the granting of an interview is intended to create an employment contract between myself and Marriott Corporation for either employment or for the providing of any benefit. No promises regarding continued employment have been made to me, and I understand that no such promises or guarantee is binding upon Marriott unless made in writing.

PLEASE SIGN HERE _____ DATE _____

*Marriott does not discriminate in hiring or employment on the basis of race, color, religion, national origin, sex, age, disability, or veteran status. No question on this application is intended to secure information to be used for such discrimination. If you are a qualified veteran and would like to be considered under Marriott's Affirmative Action Program, please inform us.

THIS APPLICATION WILL RECEIVE ACTIVE CONSIDERATION FOR THIRTY DAYS

This inquiry is **PROHIBITED** in the following states:

CALIFORNIA   OHIO
NEW YORK   PENNSYLVANIA
MASSACHUSETTS   MAINE

Applicants applying for positions located in the above referred states should **NOT** answer these questions.

• JUST FOR **FUN** •

Answer each question below. Then, fit each answer into the crossword puzzle. The first word is done for you. Your teacher has the answers.

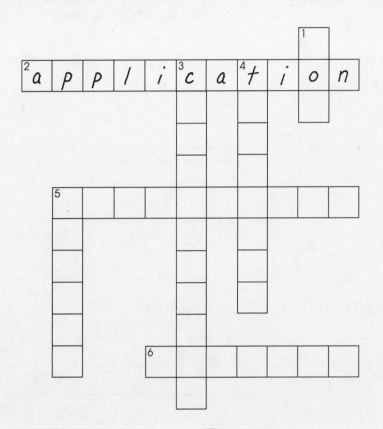

Across

2. The job _application_ is one of the most important forms you will ever fill out.

5. Employers often ask you to list three _____, or people who can verify your work.

6. A _____ is a group of people you use as a resource, to tell you about job openings.

Down

1. If you fill out a job application neatly and completely, you have a better chance at getting the ____.

3. When you send an employer your resume, you should also send a

_____ _____

to explain what job you are applying for.

4. If you have been trained to use special job skills, you would list these skills under the _____ heading on your resume.

5. A _____ is a one-page summary of your best skills and strengths.

Application Know-How

You have worked hard in this unit. Filling out a job application takes time and effort. There may be something you need to work on to help you improve your application skills.

In the space below, tell about a problem you have had with filling out job applications. How will you solve this problem?

Problem:

_____

_____

_____

How to solve it:

_____

_____

_____

_____

_____

INTERVIEWING
UNIT FIVE

Putting Your Best Foot Forward

In the last unit, you learned how to fill out job applications. After you have applied for a job, the employer may call you for an **interview**. An interview is a meeting you have with an employer about a job. Not all people who apply for a job get an interview. Employers only interview people they may want to hire.

How This Unit Will Help You

The interview lets the employer learn more about you. It also lets you learn more about the job and the employer. This unit will help you work on your interview skills.

In this unit you will

• sharpen your **interview skills**

• find out how to handle tough interview **questions**

• go through a **practice interview**

• learn how to write **thank-you notes**

Before the Interview

As you get ready for your interview, keep in mind these points:

Interviewer wants to know

- Can you do the job?
- Will you fit in?
- Will you stay?
- Are you dependable?

You want to know

- What is the job really like?
- What is expected of me?
- What is working here like?
- Is this the best job for me?

What should you wear?
You want to look good, but without calling attention to your appearance. Wear clothes a little better than those you would wear on the job. You may interview at a company where most people wear jeans to work. You could wear good slacks or a skirt to the interview.

Avoid: sneakers and sandals, T-shirts, shorts, flashy clothes, or too much jewelry or makeup. Above all, be clean and neat—and look sharp!

Getting ready means more than looking good. You need to prepare. Before an interview, you should know

- the date, time, and place of the interview
- how you will get to the interview
- the name of the person you will meet
- what you want to learn about the job
- what you want the employer to know about you

Before an interview, it is helpful to learn what you can about the company and its business.

At the Interview

The interview is very important to both you and the employer. At an interview, you both want to learn two things:

1. Are you the right person for the job? *and, if so,*

2. Is this the right job for you to take?

To answer these questions, both you and the interviewer need more information. The interview will help each of you get that information.

Try to relax. Think about your strengths. Remember, you got the interview because the company is interested in you.

You already know you should dress well and look good. How you act in an interview is also very important. Below are some *Do's* and *Don'ts* to remember:

Do	**Don't**
• go alone	• eat, smoke, or chew gum
• ask how to pronounce the interviewer's name, if you are not sure	• be afraid to ask questions
	• talk on, and on, and on . . .
• relax, smile, be friendly	• say anything negative
• keep eye contact with the interviewer when you talk	• wear a hat, outdoor coat, or sunglasses during the interview
• be honest, and be yourself	• use the interviewer's first name
• show that you are interested	• ask about pay, vacations, or other benefits until you are offered the job, or before the interviewer brings it up
• "sell" yourself	

Picture Perfect

Look at the two pictures below.

This first picture shows a woman in an interview. Notice how she is dressed and what she is doing. She will probably make a good impression on the interviewer.

Now look at this picture. What is wrong with the way the woman looks? What is wrong with what she is doing? Find at least four mistakes she is making.

Directions

Step 1. Draw a line to each mistake.

Step 2. Then, write what she should have done instead.

Here is an example: *Come alone to the interview.*

1. _____

2. _____

3. _____

4. _____

Answering Questions

The next few pages show scenes from interviews. The scenes show some common kinds of questions you may be asked in any job interview. In each scene, look at the question the interviewer is asking Sue.

Scene 1

This is an **open-ended** question. Open-ended questions have no one correct answer. Questions like these give Sue a chance to tell more about herself. She is careful to say only what will help her get this job.

Directions
Below are some open-ended questions you might hear in an interview. Think about your job choice. Pick at least one question to answer.

"What is your work history?"

_____

_____

"Would you tell me about yourself?"

_____

_____

"Why do you want this job or want to work for this company?"

_____

_____

Handling a Tough Question

Scene 2

Mr. Weller has Sue's resume and application in a folder on his desk. His company needs dependable people.

"Sue, I see from your application that you worked all last year. How many days of work did you miss during the year?" Mr. Weller asks.

Sue knows that employers need people they can count on. On her last job, she had been absent only a few days. She was sick three days, and once she had to stay home with her son. She knows she is a good, dependable worker.

"I missed only a few days because of illness," she answers. "I am always on time, and I get my work done."

Mr. Weller likes Sue's answer. He knows that people miss work from time to time. Sue's answer shows that she is dependable.

Questions

1. Why do you think Mr. Weller asked about Sue's absences?

_____

_____

_____

2. Do you think Sue was honest in her answer?

_____

_____

_____

3. Do you think Sue showed she is dependable?

_____

_____

4. What did Sue say that pointed out her strengths?

_____

_____

Answers

1. his company needs dependable people, and he wants to be sure that Sue is not absent often   2. and 3. answers will vary   4. "I am always on time, and I get my work done."

Be Confident

Scene 3

Even though Sue's work experience and skills are on her resume, she is asked about them. The same thing may happen to you. Try to give real-life examples. Show that you are confident that you can do the job.

Directions
Below are some self-confidence questions that you might hear in an interview. Think about your job choice. Pick at least one question to answer.

"What are your strengths?"

_____

_____

_____

"Why should we hire you?"

_____

_____

_____

"Why are you the best person for the job?"

_____

_____

_____

You Be the Interviewer

In an interview, it is important for you to learn more about the job and the company. You will learn some of these things when you prepare for the interview. You will probably learn more from what the interviewer tells you. But you should know what things you want to learn about.

Near the end of most interviews, you will be asked if *you* have any questions. You should have questions, and you should ask them. Asking questions helps you in two ways:

1. It gives you a chance to learn things about the job or the company.

2. It shows the interviewer that you are interested in the company.

What Questions Should You Ask?
Below are some questions you might want to ask:

- "What is your policy on promotions?"

- "What about working weekends or overtime?"

- "How will I get trained to learn new skills?"

What are some other questions you might want to ask? Write them below.

_____

_____

_____

_____

_____

Hiring Me Will Help You!

Remember, the interviewer wants to know how you can help the company. The idea you want to leave with the interviewer is "Hiring ME will help YOU!"

Directions
Think about interviewing for a job that you want. Remember the motto "Hiring ME will help YOU!" Answer these questions.

1. What do you want to know about the job?

_____

_____

_____

2. What do you want the interviewer to know about you?

_____

_____

_____

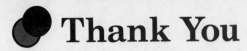

Thank You

You have learned a lot about interviewing. There is still one more step. Always send a thank-you letter or note to the interviewer within three days after the interview. The purpose of the note is

- to help the interviewer remember you

- to show that you are still interested in the job

- to be courteous

The note should be short and to the point. Sending a thank-you card (you can buy small packets of these) with a handwritten note inside is fine.

Here is an example of a thank-you note:

Thank You!

Dear Mr. Weller,

    I enjoyed talking with you last Monday and learning more about Technology, Inc. I like the way the company is growing and making new products. My career goals are to learn new skills and grow with the technology industry. The electronic parts assembly position we discussed seems like a great place to begin.

    I look forward to seeing you soon. Thank you again.

Sincerely,

Sue Robinson

Sue Robinson

Practice Interview

Now that you have read about interviews, it is time to do a practice interview.

Directions

Step 1. Get together with another person in your class. If this is not possible, see if a family member can help you out. Decide who will be the interviewer, and who will be interviewed.

Step 2. Read through each item below. Then, begin your interview.

The Interviewer
- Find out what position the person is applying for.

- Choose five questions from the interview questions listed on pages 69–72.

- Introduce yourself. Greet the person with a handshake and a smile.

- Use the interview rating sheet on page 77 to give the person feedback on his or her interview. Note this person's best qualities.

The Person Being Interviewed
- Be ready to tell the interviewer what position you want to apply for.

- Look over your answers to the interview questions on pages 69–72.

- Decide which of your skills you will mention during the interview.

- Look over the questions on page 73. Decide which questions you will ask this interviewer.

- RELAX. Introduce yourself. Greet the interviewer with a handshake and a smile.

Step 3. Take time to go over the interview rating sheet.

Step 4. Next, trade places. Repeat all of the steps above.

Interview Rating Sheet

Name of person being interviewed: _____

Name of interviewer: _____

Directions
Rate the person being interviewed on a scale of 1 to 5,
with 5 being the highest. Circle the number that seems
the closest.

	needs practice	fair	very good
Gave a clear introduction	1—–—2———	3———4	——–5
Made good eye contact	1—–—2———	3———4	——–5
Seemed to be interested in the job	1—–—2———	3———4	——–5
Knew his or her strengths	1—–—2———	3———4	——–5
Gave examples when answering questions	1—–—2———	3———4	——–5
Could answer hard questions	1—–—2———	3———4	——–5
Seemed able to do the job	1—–—2———	3———4	——–5
Asked good questions	1—–—2———	3———4	——–5
Would be interesting to work with	1—–—2———	3———4	——–5

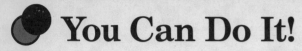

You Can Do It!

Interviewing for a job is an important step. People often get nervous when they go to a job interview. This is normal. However, it is important to find ways to interview well.

In the space below, tell about a problem you have with interviewing for a job. How will you solve the problem?

Problem:

_____

_____

_____

How to solve it:

_____

_____

_____

_____

Succeeding on Your Job

In this book, you have learned a process to get the job that is right for you. In this last unit, you will look at on-the-job success. You will look at **keeping** a job and at **getting ahead** on the job.

Keeping a job takes effort—it can be hard. You need to know what your employer wants and expects from you. You must work hard to meet those expectations.

Getting ahead means doing more than just the job. Employers promote people who work hard, take responsibility, and learn new skills.

How This Unit Will Help You

If you know what employers expect from you, you can decide whether you want to get ahead on the job.

In this unit you will

- learn about your **rights** and **responsibilities**
- find out what employers will **expect** of you
- learn how to **keep** a job
- learn ways to **get ahead** on the job

Al's Story

EQUAL
OPPORTUNITY
EMPLOYER

It was Al's first day on the job as a baker's assistant. He met with the owner, Mr. Stein. "Al, let's get started," Mr. Stein said. "Before you begin working, there are many things you need to do."

Mr. Stein took Al to the personnel office. There, Ms. Jones asked Al to fill out an employee information form. He listed his name, address, social security number, and date of birth. He also had to fill out a form called *Who to Contact in Case of Emergency.*

Next, Ms. Jones gave Al a W-4 form to fill out. She said, "The W-4 tells how much income tax should be taken out of your paycheck." Al also needed to join the union. His union dues would come out of his pay, too.

As Al left, Ms. Jones said, "Be sure to read this employee handbook. It tells about our employment and probation policies. If you do good work during your first three months, you will become a regular employee. That means that you can get the health insurance benefits and a raise of one dollar per hour."

Mr. Stein said, "That's right. We want you to do well here. Please read the company rules and the safety policy in the employee handbook. You need to work the hours that the company needs you. Your shift is 6:00 A.M. to 3:00 P.M. Let's go meet Jack, your supervisor."

"OK, Mr. Stein," Al said. "I am looking forward to working here."

They found Jack by the bread racks. "Jack will train you on your new job," said Mr. Stein. "If you have any questions, be sure to ask him. Jack will check your work and tell you how you're doing."

Jack showed Al what he was supposed to do. "Al," he said, "we have a good crew here. I hope you'll fit in and enjoy your work."

"I'm sure I will," said Al.

Questions About the Story

Circle the letter of your answer choice.

1. Where did Mr. Stein take Al on his first day?

    a. to the personnel office

    b. to take a drug test

    c. to work

2. What did Al do in the personnel office?

    a. he visited with his co-workers

    b. he filled out forms

    c. he ate lunch

3. What does *probation* mean to Al?

    a. he might go to jail

    b. he could become a regular employee in three months

    c. he got to leave work early

4. How will Jack help Al?

    a. by training Al for the job

    b. by buying Al lunch

    c. by giving Al a ride to work

Answers

1. a 2. b 3. b 4. a

● Your Rights

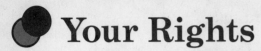

EQUAL OPPORTUNITY EMPLOYER

The personnel office at Al's bakery had a sign. It said, "Equal Opportunity Employer." This means that the employer should treat *all* employees and *all* job applicants fairly. It is good business and it's the law.

There are laws that protect workers from **discrimination**. Discrimination occurs when a worker is treated differently because of

- age
- gender, or sex (male or female)
- national origin (the country you were born in)
- race
- religion
- disabilities (any handicaps that you might have)

Equal Employment Opportunity laws require that employers treat you fairly. If you are the best-qualified person for the job, you should be hired or promoted.

When you apply for a job,

- interviewing must be fair
- testing must be fair

When you work on the job,

- you must get the same pay as others doing the same work
- you must get the same benefits as others doing the same work
- you must get an equal chance to get ahead

Where to Get Help

If you have been treated unfairly, you should file a complaint with the U.S. Equal Employment Opportunity Commission. Each area of the country has an office you can call for help. Someone at the commission in your area will help you decide if laws have been broken.

Find your state or area in the left-hand column. Your commission is located in the city listed to the right.

State Served	City	Phone Number
Alabama	Birmingham	205-731-0082
Alaska	Seattle	206-442-0968
Arizona	Phoenix	602-640-5000
Arkansas	Memphis	901-722-2617
California (northern)	San Francisco	415-744-6500
California (southern)	Los Angeles	213-251-7278
Colorado	Denver	303-866-1300
Connecticut	New York	212-264-7161
Delaware	Philadelphia	215-597-7784
Florida	Miami	305-536-4491
Georgia	Atlanta	404-331-6093
Hawaii	San Francisco	415-744-6500
Idaho	Seattle	206-442-0968
Illinois	Chicago	312-353-2713
Indiana	Indianapolis	317-226-7212
Iowa	Milwaukee	414-297-1111
Kansas	St. Louis	314-425-6585
Kentucky	Indianapolis	317-226-7212
Louisiana	New Orleans	504-589-2329
Maine	New York	212-264-7161
Maryland	Baltimore	301-962-3932
Massachusetts	New York	212-264-7161
Michigan	Detroit	313-226-7636
Minnesota	Milwaukee	414-297-1111
Mississippi	Birmingham	205-731-0082
Missouri	St. Louis	314-425-6585
Montana	Denver	303-866-1300
Nebraska	St. Louis	314-425-6585
Nevada	Los Angeles	213-251-7278
New Hampshire	New York	212-264-7161

New Jersey	Philadelphia	215-597-7784
New Mexico	Phoenix	602-640-5000
New York	New York	212-264-7161
N. Carolina	Charlotte	704-563-2501
N. Dakota	Denver	303-866-1300
Ohio	Cleveland	216-522-2001
Oklahoma	Dallas	214-767-7015
Oregon	Seattle	206-442-0968
Pennsylvania	Philadelphia	215-597-7784
Rhode Island	New York	212-264-7161
S. Carolina	Atlanta	404-331-6093
S. Dakota	Denver	303-866-1300
Tennessee	Memphis	901-722-2617
Texas (southern)	San Antonio	512-229-4810
Texas (northern)	Dallas	214-767-7015
Utah	Phoenix	602-640-5000
Vermont	New York	212-264-7161
Virginia	Baltimore	301-962-3932
Washington	Seattle	206-442-0968
W. Virginia	Philadelphia	215-597-7784
Wisconsin	Milwaukee	414-297-1111
Wyoming	Denver	303-866-1300
Other Areas	**City**	**Phone Number**
Washington, D.C.	Baltimore	301-962-3932
Panama Canal	Miami	305-536-4491
Virgin Islands	New York	212-264-7161
Puerto Rico	New York	212-264-7161
American Samoa	San Francisco	415-744-6500
Guam	San Francisco	415-744-6500
N. Marianas	San Francisco	415-744-6500
Wake Island	San Francisco	415-744-6500

Write the phone number of your Equal Employment
Opportunity Commission office here:

_ _ _ - _ _ _ - _ _ _ _

Call this number if you think you have been
discriminated against because of age, gender, nationality,
race, religion, or disabilities.

 # Responsibilities

Both you and your company have responsibilities.

Directions

Step 1. Look at each of the statements below. Decide who you think should be responsible for each statement—the worker, the company, or both.

Step 2. Put a check in the right box or boxes. The first two have been done for you.

1. follow safety rules
   - ☑ worker
   - ☐ company

2. provide a safe place to work
   - ☐ worker
   - ☑ company

3. treat all employees fairly
   - ☐ worker
   - ☐ company

4. have good work habits
   - ☐ worker
   - ☐ company

5. get along with co-workers
   - ☐ worker
   - ☐ company

6. have a good attitude
   - ☐ worker
   - ☐ company

7. provide paychecks
   - ☐ worker
   - ☐ company

8. give a job description
   - ☐ worker
   - ☐ company

9. always be on time
   - ☐ worker
   - ☐ company

10. provide training
    - ☐ worker
    - ☐ company

11. follow directions
    - ☐ worker
    - ☐ company

12. give raises and promotions
    - ☐ worker
    - ☐ company

Answers
The worker is responsible for items 1, 4, 5, 6, 9, and 11
The company is responsible for items 2, 3, 7, 8, 10, and 12

Al Makes the Grade

Al had been working at the bakery for almost three months. It was time for his work review. Mr. Stein called Al into his office. There was a work review form on Mr. Stein's desk. Al felt nervous. He had never had a work review on any job.

"Have a seat, Al," said Mr. Stein. "You've been with us for almost three months. How do you feel about your job?"

"I like my job," said Al. "I've worked hard to learn everything."

"I hear you are becoming a good baker," said Mr. Stein. "Your supervisor has filled out this work review form."

Al could see that his supervisor thought he was doing well on most things. He got good marks on knowing about his job and getting along with others. The highest mark was on his attitude. The only low mark was on work habits. Al had been late five or six times. Twice, his babysitter had been sick. Other times, he'd had car trouble.

Mr. Stein liked Al's work. "We want to make you a regular employee," he said. "However, when you're late, it causes problems for the bakery. Al, you must get to work on time."

"I'm sorry about being late. I've had problems with the babysitter and with the car. I will solve these problems right away. I know it is important to be on time."

"Good," said Mr. Stein. "We are depending on you now. Next Monday, you can sign up for health insurance. Your pay will increase by one dollar per hour. I hope you will be with us for a long time."

● Questions

1. Name two things that Al's supervisor likes about his work.

_____

_____

_____

2. What is the problem that Mr. Stein pointed out to Al?

_____

_____

_____

3. Why is it important for Al to solve his problem?

_____

_____

_____

Answers
1. knowing about his job, getting along with others, or having a good attitude 2. Al had been late five or six times. When Al is late, it causes problems for the bakery. 3. answers will vary

Al Takes Action

To be successful on a job, you need to meet your employer's expectations. Sometimes, this is easy to do. Other times, it takes a lot of your time and effort. This was the situation that Al faced.

After talking to Mr. Stein, Al knew that he had to improve his work habits if he wanted to keep his job. This meant he had to be on time every day. He had to be able to depend on his car. His raise would help him save money for car repairs.

A bigger problem was child care. Jane, his babysitter, was not very reliable. It was a real problem for Al. He called Jane that evening. She told him that she would not be able to watch his children anymore. He asked her if she knew of anyone who could take her place. She gave him the phone number of a child-care center.

Al decided to also ask his son's teacher if he knew of any babysitters. He also looked in the want ads and the yellow pages. He was determined to solve this problem.

Al was taking positive steps to succeed at his job. It was not enough for Al just to get by. He really wanted to get ahead.

● Questions

1. How did Al go about solving his babysitter problem?

_____

_____

_____

Al knew he had to solve his problems to be successful. Think about a problem in your life. Is there a problem that you need to solve to be successful on a job? For example, you may have children but no babysitter. This is a problem that you will need to solve.

2. Describe a problem that you need to solve.

_____

_____

_____

3. What will you do to solve this problem?

_____

_____

_____

Answers

1. he asked his babysitter and his son's teacher if they knew of any babysitters, he looked in the want ads and the yellow pages for babysitters. 2. and 3. answers will vary

● Getting Ahead

Al was pushing racks of bread into the storeroom. Pat was walking along behind, sweeping around the machines and tables.

Mr. Stein walked in and asked, "Hey, which one of you wants to learn how to use the new packaging machine? It means staying after work for three nights to get trained."

"Does this mean changing jobs?" Al asked. Mr. Stein explained that it was an added job responsibility.

Pat asked if it would mean a pay raise.

"Not right away," Mr. Stein replied. "Are either of you interested?"

Pat and Al looked at each other.

Now get together with another student. Talk about the offer Mr. Stein made to Pat and Al. Answer this question:

Al wants to get ahead in the bakery. What do you think he should do? Why?

Pat shrugged. He went on sweeping.

"I am interested," said Al. "I'll call my babysitter to tell her I will be late."

"Good!" said Mr. Stein. "Let's go into the packaging area."

Pat watched, and then went on sweeping. This was his last task for the day.

The next day, Al went to work early. He went into the packaging area to look over the machines again. Pat came in, on time as usual.

"Al, when did you get here?" Pat asked.

"About a half hour ago," Al answered.

"Why?" Pat asked.

Al said, "I just wanted to check what I learned about these machines."

Pat looked confused. "Why do you want more work to do?"

"I think this is a good chance to get ahead in the bakery," Al replied.

Now get together with another student. Talk about the offer Mr. Stein made to Pat and Al. Answer this question:

Al agreed to stay late to learn a new job. He did this to get ahead. How do you think Mr. Stein will feel about what Al has done?

Getting ahead on the job means

- coming in early
- doing what needs to be done
- being willing to learn new things

Can you think of others?

Congratulations!

You should feel proud of yourself. You have learned a process for getting a job.

This is a process you can use as often as you need to.

Now that you know these job-finding steps, the next step is up to you.

What do you plan to do with what you have learned? Write or draw your plans below.